North across the Border

The Story of the Mexican Americans

GREAT JOURNEYS

North across the Border

The Story of the Mexican Americans

by Lila Perl

BENCHMARK BOOKS

MARSHALL CAVENDISH
NEW YORK

For Sheri Walter
and with thanks for their lively and up-to-the-minute reporting to:
Warren Link in New Mexico
Evelyn Meyerson in California
Ruth Wolff in Colorado

Benchmark Books
Marshall Cavendish Corporation
99 White Plains Road
Tarrytown, NY 10591-9001

© 2002 by Lila Perl
Map © by Marshall Cavendish Corporation
Map by Rodica Prato

Cover photograph: *Refugees fleeing the ravages of the Mexican Revolution cross the border into the United States, April 1913.*

Photo research by Candlepants Incorporated
Cover Photo: Dept. of Special Collections, Young Research Libraries, UCLA
The photographs in this book are used by permission and through the courtesy of; *Seaver Center for Western History Research*: 2–3, 30. *The Bancroft Library, University of California, Berkeley*: 8, 20, 26, 38(right). *Library of Congress*: (#221141) 10, (lcusf34248290) 56, 63. *Dept. Of Library Services, American Museum of Natural History* (photo#326597) 13. *National Museum of American Art/Washington DC/Art Resource* NY: 16. *General Research Division, New York Public Library, Astor, Lenox and Tilden Foundation*: 18. *Schalkwijk/Art Resource* NY: 22. *Western History Collections, University of Oklahoma Libraries*: 32. *Museum of New Mexico* (photo #22468) 34. *Corbis*: Bettmann, 38 (left), 40, 45, 52, 64, 67, 78, 79, 82, 96, 75; Ted Streshinsky, 84; James A. Sugar, 86; Stephanie Maze, 88, 95, 105; Raymond Gehmond, 89; Annie Griffiths Belt, 92; Catherine Karnow, 98. Joseph Sohm Chromosohm Inc., 101; David Turnley, 103; AFP, 107. *Arizona Historical Society/Tucson*: 42, 58. *Regional History Collection, Department of Special Collections, University of Southern California*: 47. *Gersheim Collection, Harry Ransom Humanities Research Center, The University of Texas at Austin*: 48. *Houston Public Library, Metropolitan Research Center*: 55. *Los Angeles Times Photo*: 66. *F. Arturo Rosales*: 69. *Devra Weber*: 70. *Denver Public Library, Western History Collection*: 74

Library of Congress Cataloging-in-Publication Data
Perl, Lila.
North across the border: the story of the Mexican Americans / by Lila Perl.
p.   cm. — (Great journeys)
Includes bibliographical references (p.) and index.
ISBN 0-7614-1226-3
1. Mexican Americans—History—Juvenile literature. [1. Mexican Americans—History.]
I. Title. II. Great journeys (Benchmark Books (Firm))
E184.M5 P426   2002   973'.046872—dc21   00-057017

Printed in the United States of America

1 3 5 6 4 2

Contents

Also by Lila Perl

Foreword

WHEN WE THINK ABOUT IMMIGRANTS COMING TO THE UNITED STATES, we imagine long journeys across thousands of miles of open sea. We picture the first European settlers of the New World tossing perilously in their frail sailing vessels; the Irish fleeing the potato famine of the 1840s in overcrowded, disease-ridden "coffin" ships.

Like the Atlantic Ocean, the Pacific became a watery route bringing Chinese immigrants to California eager to claim their share of the gold discovered there in 1848. Once the age of steam had arrived, in the late 1800s, millions of people from eastern and southern Europe, in particular, began to stream across the Atlantic. The sailing time via steamship shortened the journey by weeks. But the distances remained great, just as they are for today's newcomers from Europe and Asia who arrive by plane.

Moctezuma, the Aztec ruler, being crowned in his palace

Yet for thousands of years the so-called New World, which was to become the Americas, was already peopled. To the highly varied and widely scattered Native Americans—the Hopi of the future southwestern United States, the Aztecs of future Mexico, the Incas of South America—it was already an "old" world in which long-established settlements and civilizations thrived.

Then to the alarm of the native population, a great change took place beginning with the appearance of a helmeted and sword-bearing people from afar, many of them mounted on the backs of strange-looking beasts known as horses. These explorers and invaders were Spaniards following the westward sea journey made in 1492 by the Spanish-commissioned Italian captain, Christopher Columbus.

Even before Jamestown was first settled in 1607, before the *Mayflower* landing of 1620, Spain had colonized many parts of the New World. By 1509, Juan Ponce de Leon had become governor of Puerto Rico and, in 1513, he claimed Florida for Spain. Diego Velásquez completed his conquest of the island of Cuba in 1514, and in 1519 Hernán Cortés landed in Mexico.

In conquering what was to become Mexico, the Spaniards imposed a new language, system of laws, religion, architecture, agriculture, and means of transportation on the Native Americans. But the indigenous peoples were not without their own cultural traditions expressed in their foods, clothing, crafts, folk customs, festivals, and means of worship.

Inevitably, the two worlds blended, as did the people themselves, to create a new mestizo (from the Spanish word for "mixed") culture that was neither wholly Spanish nor wholly native, but Mexican. It was this way of life that would be carried into the far reaches of the unbounded land that the conquerors called New Spain, and that would characterize the estimated 23 million Mexicans and Mexican Americans who live in the United States today.

The Spanish conqueror, Hernán Cortés, held sway at the court of Moctezuma, soon after his arrival in the Aztec capital.

One

The Border Is Drawn

WHEN, IN 1519, HERNÁN CORTÉS ARRIVED IN THE FUTURE MEXICO, HE had no idea of the size and terrain of the region he was about to claim for Spain. He and his party landed on the steamy Gulf Coast at what is today the city of Veracruz and had to scale steep volcanic mountains to reach the Aztec stronghold in the 6,000-foot central highlands.

News of their arrival spread quickly. As soon as the Aztec ruler Moctezuma, or Montezuma, learned of the foreigners' presence from neighboring peoples, he sent gifts to the coast. The richly fashioned articles of gold and silver confirmed the invaders' suspicions that this new land held unimaginable riches. Moctezuma's generosity drew the visitors to the Aztec capital of Tenochtitlán for they were certain that it was the site of the wealth they were seeking.

Although the Aztecs had a population of more than 300,000, they were no match for Cortés, who had originally arrived with only 500 men and 16 horses. His conquest of their empire was completed in 1521, with reinforcements totaling no more than 1,000 Spaniards, but aided by allies among the local peoples.

One explanation for the success of the Spanish conquest appears to be rooted in the Aztec religion, which had foretold the return after many years of the god Quetzalcoatl. Translated from the Náhuatl language, the name means "bird-snake," or plumed (or feathered) serpent. Was it possible, the Aztecs wondered, that Cortés, this light-skinned, bearded man, encased in shining armor and bearing swords, lances, and firearms, could be the mythic figure they had long awaited? As to the mounted Spanish warriors, they were so curious looking that at first the Aztecs believed horse and rider to be a single supernatural figure.

Another reason for Spain's conquest of the Aztecs can be traced to the resentment of neighboring peoples from whom the powerful Aztecs had been exacting labor, goods, and human lives for more than a hundred years. Particularly abhorrent to them was the Aztec practice of human sacrifice for which they were forced to provide victims. As a result, the oppressed neighbors of the Aztecs were ready to join with the Spaniards in the destruction of their oppressors.

In 1518, the year before the arrival of Cortés, the population of the territory that would be called New Spain is estimated to have numbered 25 million. Who were the people of New Spain? Dating from 1000 B.C., a succession of civilizations of artistic brilliance and advanced knowledge had risen to prominence. Among them were the Olmecs, the Zapotecs, and Mixtecs dwelling in the vicinity of Puebla and Oaxaca; the Toltecs and Chichimecs of the central highlands, later conquered by the Aztecs; and in the southeast there were the Mayans. At its height, from A.D. 300–900, the Mayan civilization was one of the most highly accomplished in the world in mathematics, astronomy, and architecture. But with the Spanish conquest of 1521, the era of Mexico's native civilizations came to a close.

The Aztec capital of Tenochtitlán, with its pyramids and grand palaces, held the promise of a land rich in the mineral wealth the Spanish invaders sought.

As for the extent of New Spain, it was as little known to the new Spanish overlords as was the history of its inhabitants. Even the first Spanish viceroy, appointed in 1535, had no idea of the size of the domain over which he ruled.

Spain's greed for mineral wealth, however, was so great that is was not long before the Spanish explorer Francisco Vásquez de Coronado headed north in search of the fabled Seven Cities of Cíbola, said to be glittering with gold and emeralds. In 1540 he set out with a force of armed Spaniards and *indios*, as the native peoples were called. His expedition reached present-day Arizona and New Mexico, and parts of Texas,

Oklahoma, and Kansas. Some of his men even got to see the Grand Canyon. But nowhere in the future American Southwest did Coronado find the riches he sought. He found the Hopi living on the high, barren mesas of northern Arizona, and the Zuñis whose mud-brick, or adobe, huts hugged the terraced lands in New Mexico.

The despair of Coronado's soldiers who searched in vain for the Seven Cities of Cíbola is described in the following account written in 1598 by Gaspar Pérez de Villagrá in his *History of New Mexico*.

Because they did not stumble over bars of gold and silver immediately upon commencing their march into these regions, and because the streams and lakes and springs they met flowed crystalline waters instead of liquid golden victuals, they cursed the barren land and cried out bitterly against those who had led them into such a wilderness. Complaining and bewailing their fate, more like women than men, they left all behind and turned their backs upon the expedition they had begun. It is well to pause here rather than to continue the details of such a shameful tale.

Although Coronado did not return with the treasures he had expected, his journey was not a complete loss. All the lands he had explored were claimed by the Spaniards, adding to their vast holdings in the New World. Starting in 1598 Spain's grip on the region was tightened by Juan de Oñate, who traversed a similar route. After crossing the Rio Grande at the future site of El Paso, Texas, he established a settlement near present-day Santa Fe. The Spaniards called this territory Nuevo México, a name they had adapted from the Aztecs, who were also known as the Méxica.

Soon after the conquest of New Spain, the Spanish laid claim to California. In 1542 Juan Rodríguez Cabrillo sailed up the coast to a point beyond San Francisco Bay. Little did he know that three hundred years would pass before the wealth so coveted by Spain would be discovered in

California or that, by then, Spain would have lost its largest possession in North America.

A MAJOR ASPECT OF SPANISH RULE IN THE NEW WORLD WAS THE CONversion of its native peoples to the Roman Catholic faith. Priests and missionaries frequently accompanied the military, giving rise to the oft-repeated comment that Spain conquered with "the cross and the sword."

In 1531, the transition from the Aztec religion to Christianity was aided by a miraculous event. A recently converted Native American who had taken the name of Juan Diego reported having seen the Virgin Mary on a hill called Tepeyac on the outskirts of today's Mexico City. According to the fifty-five-year-old Diego, the Virgin had appeared to him amidst blooming roses on a spot where only cactus had previously grown.

At her request, Diego filled his cloak with roses and presented himself to the bishop. When he opened his cloak, the roses had disappeared. In their place was an image of the Virgin imprinted on the cloth.

A church was built on the site of Diego's vision and its date, December 12, became the Day of Our Lady of Guadalupe, patron saint of Mexico. Ever since, Mexicans and Mexican Americans have celebrated Guadalupe Day as a religious feast with church masses, fairs, and fireworks.

The new faith was accepted by many of the former worshippers of the numerous Aztec gods. The churches had their own religious images and towering or domed architecture, plus painted and gilded altars. Just as the Aztecs had once reverently ascended the pyramids, they would, as time passed, approach the Shrine of Guadalupe inch by inch on their knees.

Along with the new religion, the conquered peoples were yoked to an economic arrangement that reduced them, almost without exception, to a condition of near-slavery. Under a system known as the *encomienda*, the viceroys of New Spain gave large tracts of land for agriculture and mining to wealthy Spaniards, members of both the aristocracy and the clergy. In return for their services, the serflike workers were paid little or

The appearance of the Virgin of Guadalupe to Juan Diego helped establish the Christian faith in Mexico.

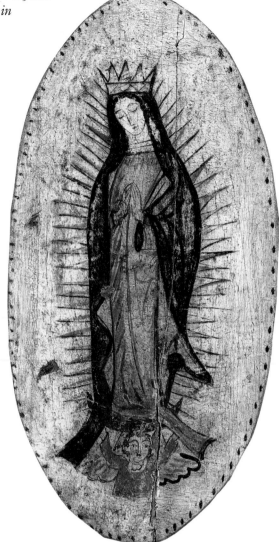

nothing by their masters. The Spanish *patrón* was required to feed and clothe and see to the spiritual needs of his laborers only as he saw fit.

Another institution that was highly abusive to the native peoples was the *repartimiento*, the rounding up of *indios* for forced labor on special jobs such as clearing land or building roads. Both of these practices were harshly criticized by a compassionate Spanish priest, Bartolomé de las

Casas who succeeded in getting laws passed in 1542 that were intended to reduce the atrocities taking place on the haciendas, or farming estates, and in the gold, silver, copper, and lead mines. But in actuality few changes for the better ensued.

Although the harsh treatment of the native population caused many deaths, most fatalities occurred as a result of European-introduced diseases, such as measles and smallpox, to which the *indios* had no immunity. It is estimated that by 1550 the population of New Spain had been reduced from 25 million, in 1518, to 6 million. Yet, the native population remained large enough to provide the necessary labor force. And, unlike the lands Spain controlled in the Caribbean Sea, where black slaves had to be imported for field work, few Africans were brought to New Spain.

The society of the new colony soon developed a rigid class structure. At the top of the ladder—socially, politically, and economically—were the "pure" Spanish overlords who had been born in Spain and were known as *peninsulares*. But what did "pure" Spanish really mean? The Spaniards themselves were a mix of Iberians plus Phoenicians, Greeks, Carthaginians, and Romans from the Mediterranean basin. Added to this intermingling were Germanic tribes as well as Jews and Moorish peoples from the Near East.

Just a step beneath the *peninsulares* were the *criollos*, or Creoles, who were the offspring of "pure" Spanish parents, but who had been born in New Spain. Next came the mestizos, products of Spanish and native intermarriage, and lastly the *indios* or Native Americans, large pockets of which remained hidden in the southern jungles and in remote mountain and desert areas.

THE RIGID CLASS STRUCTURE OF NEW SPAIN HAD A FAR-REACHING EFFECT. It served to strengthen both the church and the hacienda system and to fuse the two as a means of colonizing both the heartland and its northern territories.

Mestizos, people of mixed Spanish and native birth, and criollos, *Spaniards born in Mexico, soon made up a large portion of the population.*

During the 1600s and 1700s scores of agricultural settlements, known as missions, were built north of the Rio Grande in Texas, in the New Mexico territory, and in California. The missions were run by the priesthood, worked by *indios* and mestizos, and fortified against attack by the Spanish military presence. The mission buildings included a church, housing for the clergy, and more humble dwellings for the converts of *indio* or mestizo birth. It was their job to care for the Spanish-imported cattle or flocks of sheep, and to tend the crops, many of which—such as wheat and other grains, fruits, and vegetables—had been brought to the New World from Europe by the Spanish colonizers.

In California twenty-one missions were built, starting in San Diego and reaching all the way to Sonoma, north of San Francisco. The California missions were roughly one day's walk apart along a trail known as El Camino Real, the royal highway. In the New Mexico territory, which included Arizona, there were about twenty-five mission settlements, some of which also operated mines that did not yield gold or precious stones but were a source of valuable minerals. A Spanish priest, Father Jeronimo de Zarate Salmerón described the life of a typical settlement in 1626.

Concerning the quality of the land, it is cold and healthful, with the climate of Spain. Its healthfulness is attested by the fact that the Indians reach the age of more than 100 years, for I have seen them. It is a fertile land with fine crystalline waters and much major and minor livestock is raised, and if it were not for the greediness of the governors who have taken them all out to sell, the fields would now be covered with them. A great supply of wheat and corn and all kinds of vegetables is gathered.

As far as saying that it is poor, I answer that there never has been discovered in the world a land with more mines of every quality, good and bad, than in New Mexico. . . . We have seen silver, copper, lead, magnet stone, alum, sulphur, and turquoise mines that the Indians work with their talent, since for them, they are diamonds and precious stones. The Spaniards who are there laugh at all this . . . which is a great deal for Spaniards, who for cause of greediness for silver and gold will enter Hell itself to obtain them.

Texas, with its broad plains, became the site of many cattle ranches as well as missions, and the Native Americans and mestizo ranch hands were the first vaqueros, or cowboys. Although the native peoples had not

The central feature of each of the Spanish missions was its church, surrounded by outbuildings for the development of agriculture, ranching, or mining operations. Pictured here is the mission at San Buena Ventura in California.

encountered cattle or horses before the Spaniards arrived, they proved expert at roping, branding, and herding. Spanish words such as *la riata* have become lariat in English, *el lazo* became lasso, and the word *vaquero* would evolve into buckaroo.

The mission system might have populated the northern reaches of New Spain much more heavily if not for a problem between the *criollos* and the Spanish crown, which escalated in the early 1800s. For some time, the Spanish colonials had felt that they were unfairly taxed, being forced to yield one-fifth of New Spain's gems and precious metals to the mother country. In addition to having to contribute the "king's fifth," the colony was forbidden to grow grapes or olives, to mine salt, or to establish a silk industry. Wine, olive oil, salt, and silk had to be purchased exclusively from Spain.

The Revolutionary War in the United States and the French Revolution undoubtedly inspired a fervor for independence throughout much of New Spain. And on September 16, 1810, a *criollo* priest, Father Miguel Hidalgo y Castillo, issued an impassioned call to arms. Vowing to overthrow the *peninsulares* who were still loyal to Spain, he led a rebel army of about 80,000 *criollos* and mestizos from his parish town of Dolores along the 150-mile route to the capital.

But the rebellion was crushed, and Father Hidalgo was tried by the office of the Spanish Inquisition and executed by a firing squad in 1811. Although his severed head was displayed as a warning to others, the movement to liberate the colony from Spain continued. Yet another revolutionary priest was executed in 1815. But in 1820 a *criollo* officer in the Spanish army, Agustín de Iturbide, changed sides and took up the rebel cause, leading to complete freedom from Spanish rule in 1821. However, it is September 16, 1810, the date of Father Hidalgo's *Grito de Dolores*, or Cry of Dolores, that is celebrated as Mexico's Independence Day.

"SO FAR FROM GOD, SO CLOSE TO THE UNITED STATES." THIS LAMENT would prove to be prophetic with regard to the northern lands held by the newly independent nation of Mexico. Drained of its wealth by its former masters, denied the power of Spain's military presence, and weakened by instability within, Mexico was ill prepared to deal with the threat that came from across the Rio Grande—the loss of the vast territory of Texas.

At first the United States offered to purchase the valuable acreage of the Mexican-held—and named—Tejas. But, in spite of the growing number of Anglo, or English-speaking, settlers that pioneer Stephen Austin and others had been leading into Texas since 1822, Mexico refused.

The Mexican priest Father Hidalgo raised the cry of rebellion against Spain that was to bring about independence for Mexico.

By 1835, there were 30,000 Anglo Americans and a few thousand African slaves in the region, overshadowing its 5,000 Mexicans. As Mexico had abolished slavery in 1829, it opposed its presence in the territory. Tensions also mounted because Mexico required all those living in Tejas to become Roman Catholics.

The Anglos rebelled and seized Mexican garrisons including the abandoned chapel of the mission known as the Alamo, which had been founded at San Antonio in 1718. In February and March 1836, the Mexicans under President General Antonio López de Santa Anna counterattacked, laying siege to and then storming the mission, an action that took the lives of nearly all the defenders. To the rallying cry, "Remember the Alamo!" the Anglos regrouped and, in a surprise battle on April 21, 1836, wrenched Texas free of Mexico. Texas remained an independent republic until 1845, when it was admitted as the twenty-eighth state.

As a result of the annexation of Texas, Mexico broke off relations with the United States. It had warned that such a step would be construed as an act of war and, by 1846, the two nations were locked in battle. Mexico, its treasury depleted and its ill-equipped forces made up largely of peasant conscripts, faced the vigorous nation to the north in what became known as the Mexican War.

Bloody raids were carried out by both sides, with General Santa Anna eventually placed in command in the hopes of a last-ditch Mexican victory. But the American forces, superior in tactics and weaponry, fought their way into the Mexican capital and the country was forced to surrender. On February 2, 1848, Mexico signed the Treaty of Guadalupe Hidalgo, at a site just outside Mexico City. According to the terms of the treaty, Mexico ceded to the United States most of the Arizona–New Mexico territory, most of the present-day states of California, Nevada, and Utah, and parts of Wyoming and Colorado. Along with the Texas annexation of 1845, this territory made up nearly half of prewar Mexico.

Practically overnight, at least 80,000 Mexicans found themselves liv-

The Treaty of Guadalupe Hidalgo

Article VIII

Mexicans now established in territories previously belonging to Mexico, and which remain for the future within the limits of the United States, as defined by the present Treaty, shall be free to continue where they now reside, or to remove at any time to the Mexican Republic, retaining the property which they possess in the said territories, or disposing thereof and removing the proceeds wherever they please; without their being subjected, on this account, to any contribution, tax or charge whatever.

Those who shall prefer to remain in the said territories, may either retain the title and rights of Mexican citizens, or acquire those of citizens of the United States. But, they shall be under the obligation to make their election within one year from the date of the exchange of ratifications of this treaty: and those who shall remain in the said territories, after the expiration of that year, without having declared their intention to retain the character of Mexicans, shall be considered to have elected to become citizens of the United States.

In said territories, property of every kind, now belonging to Mexicans not established there, shall be inviolably respected. The present owners, the heirs of these, and all Mexicans who may hereafter acquire said property by contract, shall enjoy with respect to it, guaranties equally ample as if the same belonged to citizens of the United States.

Article IX

The Mexicans who, in the territories aforesaid, shall not preserve the character of citizens of the Mexican Republic, conformably with what is stipulated in the preceding article, shall be incorporated into the Union of the United States and be admitted, at the proper time (to be judged of by the Congress of the United States) to the enjoyment of all the rights of citizens of the United States according to the principles of the Constitution; and in the mean time shall be maintained and protected in the free enjoyment of their liberty and property, and secured in the free exercise of their religion without restriction.

ing in what became the United States—approximately 60,000 in New Mexico and Arizona, 13,000 in California, and 7,000 in Texas. Some were wealthy Spanish landowners, the *ricos*. But most were *indios* or mestizos. What provisions were made for these new inhabitants of the United States?

On paper, the Treaty of Guadalupe Hidalgo offered a number of generous guarantees. Mexicans could continue to reside where they were, retain their property rights, enjoy religious and cultural freedom, and even become U.S. citizens.

But it soon became evident that in practice the provisions of the treaty would never be honored. Deep prejudices had existed for some time in the United States against both Spaniards and Native Americans. Hatred of the Spanish went all the way back to Elizabethan England with its anti-Spain, anti-Catholic attitudes that were later transplanted to American soil by the English colonists.

Inevitably the prejudices of the Anglos led to overt racist policies and discrimination by state and local authorities in the ceded territory. Although the Mexican government made repeated protests to officials in Washington, D.C., their complaints were ignored.

As for the Mexican Americans, they could justly claim, "We never crossed the border; the border crossed us." But their Anglo neighbors would continue to view them as interlopers and would exploit and oppress them far into the future.

By 1849, the discovery of gold in California was drawing prospectors from far and wide.

Two

Lost Lands and Broken Promises

GOLD WAS DISCOVERED ALONG THE SOUTH FORK OF THE AMERICAN River at Sutter's Mill in California on January 24, 1848, a mere nine days before Mexico was forced to sign the treaty that ceded California to the United States. Even if the frenzy of the 1849 gold rush that was to follow could have been foreseen, there was nothing Mexico could have done to hold onto its lost territory. Nor could it have prevented the hasty adoption of California, which was granted statehood one year later, on September 9, 1850.

At the time of the discovery of that golden nugget in the clear waters of the mill race, Sutter's Fort, about 45 miles away, was an outpost in a remote and sparsely settled region of north-central California. However, Mexicans and Native Americans were already engaged in many of the fort's enterprises—wheat farming, fur trapping, lumbering, and cattle ranching, the latter mainly for the export of tallow and hides. Other

Mexicans who had inhabited parts of the territory for so long that they called themselves Californios owned large haciendas or operated small family farms in the fertile valleys.

Despite the slow pace at which news traveled in the 1840s, gold prospectors began arriving in California with amazing speed. Those from the eastern United States either journeyed overland, made their way by boat around Cape Horn, or shortened the sailing by slogging through the steamy jungles of Panama. Still others were the crews of foreign vessels that docked at Pacific ports. Hearing of the gold strike, they jumped ship and headed inland.

Mexican citizens, particularly those who worked in the gold and silver mines of Sonora, the mountainous Mexican state below the new border, also took off for the California gold fields. Experienced miners, the Mexicans were more skilled than most of the other prospectors. They taught the Anglos how to use the *batea*, a flat-bottomed pan with sloping sides, to sift the gold out of the rivers and streams. And their experience was particularly helpful when it came to the more difficult chore of extracting veins of the precious metal from ore-bearing rock. But as the Mexicans began to arrive, often with their families, in increasing numbers, and to establish mining claims, California's Anglos grew wary.

In April 1850, the new California legislature passed the Foreign Miners' Tax Law, which was clearly aimed at the Mexican gold miners. The law levied a then-exorbitant $20 a month head tax on all non-U.S. citizens engaged in mining in California. Its sponsor, a state senator named Thomas Jefferson Green, declared that he could "maintain a better stomach at the killing of a Mexican than at the crushing of a body louse."

Such public expressions of prejudice, coupled with the passage of the new law, led to direct attacks on Mexican property. Valid Mexican mining claims were jumped, or illegally seized, by Anglos, resulting in acts of violence on both sides.

The slur "greaser," believed to derive from the hide and tallow trade

to fight against our enemies, in compliance with the requirements of that Sovereign Majesty, who, from this day forward, will hold us under His protection. On my part, I am ready to offer myself as a sacrifice for your happiness.

But matching violence with violence proved a shortsighted means of seeking change. Cortina was forced to flee Texas in 1860 and the Tejanos, having gradually lost their land to Anglo cotton growers and cattle ranchers, withdrew to southern Texas close to the border with Mexico.

A more hospitable place of residence for Mexican Americans in the mid-1800s was New Mexico, which the United States was to administer as a territory for many decades after the Mexican War. There was little mystery as to why New Mexico would not achieve statehood until 1912. It had the largest Mexican-American population in the Southwest: 60,000 Hispanos—as they were then called—versus a few thousand Anglos. (The word *Hispano* later evolved into "Hispanic," meaning of Spanish cultural heritage.)

In deferring statehood for New Mexico, the U.S. government hoped that in time enough Anglos would move into the territory to take over the ownership of its lands, mining operations, and yet-to-be-built railroads. However, an Anglo majority was slow to develop. In the meantime, the Hispanos, many of whom were exclusively of Spanish heritage rather than mestizo, began using Spanish in public documents and in courts of law. They served on juries, ran for public office, and ensured the universal right to vote. As a result, the state of New Mexico would lead the way in electing Hispanics to the U.S. Senate.

The Territory of New Mexico was enlarged in 1853 when the United States bought an additional tract of land located on its southern border with Mexico. This acquisition, known as the Gadsden Purchase, was envisioned as a profitable rail route to the Pacific coast by its sponsor, railroad promoter James Gadsden.

A Hispano farm family in New Mexico, where Anglo oppression was less severe because of the predominantly Mexican population in the territory

Ten years later, in 1863, the federal government separated New Mexico into two parts, naming the newly created western portion the Territory of Arizona. With its tiny population of about 4,000, including Hispanos, Anglos were able to dominate the territorial government. By the time statehood was granted to Arizona in 1912, the same year as New Mexico, its Hispanic peoples enjoyed fewer rights and protections than did those in New Mexico.

MEXICAN LANDS
CEDED TO THE UNITED STATES

WASHINGTON

OREGON

MONTANA

IDAHO

NEVADA

WYOMING

MEXICAN CESSION
1848

CALIFORNIA

UTAH

COLORADO

NORTH
DAKOTA

SOUTH DAKOTA

NEBRASKA

KANSAS

MINNESOTA

IOWA

MISSOURI

PACIFIC OCEAN

ARIZONA

NEW MEXICO

OKLAHOMA

ARKANSAS

GADSDEN
PURCHASE
1853

TEXAS
ANNEXATION
1845

LOUISIANA

TEXAS

MEXICO

GULF OF MEXICO

In less than ten years, major portions of Mexican territory were ceded to the United States.

As to the other spoils of the Texas Annexation and the Mexican Cession—Nevada, Utah, Colorado, Wyoming, Kansas, and Oklahoma—their Hispanic populations were small during the 1850s. Yet the pattern of repression and diminishing rights would soon become well established in these future states.

DISCOURAGED BY BROKEN PROMISES AND LIMITED OPPORTUNITIES IN THE Southwest, many Mexican citizens chose to remain on their own side of the border during the 1860s and 1870s. After twenty-two years under the inept political and military guidance of General Antonio López de Santa Anna—who had managed to lose both Texas and the Mexican War—a reform movement gained momentum.

With great hope Mexicans looked to Benito Juárez, a Zapotec of humble origin from the state of Oaxaca, who cut a Lincolnesque figure in his somber black suit and stovepipe hat. Like Abraham Lincoln, Juárez had studied law as a young man. Later he rose to government posts and, in 1861—the same year that Lincoln became president of the United States—he took office as president of Mexico.

Juárez's La Reforma policies aimed to improve the distribution of wealth by curbing the influence of the clergy and *criollos* who dominated the economy of Mexico, while its vast majority of native peoples and mestizos lived in poverty. Among the main goals of the reform movement were the separation of church and state and the redistribution of Mexico's agricultural land, nearly half of which was owned by the church.

The Juárez presidency had the support of the United States. American officials believed a successful reform movement would stem further migration north across the border. If not for the onset of the American Civil War in 1861, Juárez might have had financial help as well as moral support from Washington.

As it turned out, Juárez's government was so deeply in debt to foreign powers that the church and the landowners, hoping to unseat him, permitted the army of Emperor Napoleon III of France to enter the country. In a fierce battle at Puebla, Mexico, on May 5, 1862, Juárez's reformist army overcame the French. The fifth of May, Cinco de Mayo, still ranks as a major Mexican holiday and is celebrated along with September 16, Mexican Independence Day, by Mexicans everywhere.

Unfortunately the success of Cinco de Mayo was only temporary. Two years later, in 1864, the French established control and installed the Austrian archduke, Maximilian, as "Emperor of Mexico." Maximilian's unlikely "empire" lasted three years. Once the American Civil War ended, the United States invoked the Monroe Doctrine—guaranteeing independent nations in the Western Hemisphere freedom from European interference—and provided funds for Juárez to drive out the French. With the execution of the ill-fated Maximilian in 1867, Juárez returned to the presidency. Until his death in 1872, he tried to rebuild Mexico's shattered economy and to ensure that his religious and agricultural reforms would endure.

However, the next Mexican leader of prominence, Porfirio Díaz, was to restore many of the privileges of the *ricos* and the church. Although Díaz was a mestizo and onetime supporter of La Reforma, he looked to industrial and technological development as the key to Mexican prosperity. There would have been nothing wrong with this policy except that Díaz's development of railroads, telecommunications, and electric power turned out to benefit the land barons, the new industrialists, and the foreign investors, most of whom were Americans. Even the wealth derived from stripping the country's timber and its silver and copper reserves did not trickle down to improve the lives of the landless peasantry that made up 90 percent of the rural population. Nor did the discovery of oil on Mexico's Gulf Coast create job opportunities for the poor and the unemployed.

Throughout the *porfiriato*, as Díaz's thirty-four-year regime—from 1877 to 1911—was known, Mexico was patrolled by a military force

President Benito Juárez, a man of humble beginnings who envisioned reforms that would better the lives of Mexico's poor

The Mexican leader Porfirio Díaz, whose thirty-four-year regime overturned most of the Juárez reforms, bled the nation's resources and set the stage for the Revolution of 1910.

known as the *rurales*. These mounted and well-armed policemen roamed the countryside in search of bandits, outlaws, and the political enemies of the dictator Díaz. They also terrorized the workers who ran away from the haciendas, miners who dared protest low wages and slave-labor conditions, and any villagers found harboring weapons.

By the time Díaz, then more than eighty years old, was unseated, the stage was set for revolution. The hard-won reforms of the Juárez presidency had been overturned. Industrial development had only widened the gap between the *ricos* and the poor. And a host of idealists and reformers, militarists and bandit-generals, who thought they had the solution to Mexico's problems, were all too ready to take control. Their efforts would only create a situation that grew more chaotic as time passed.

What came to be known as the Revolution of 1910 was an era rather than a single event, lasting into the 1920s. Land reformers and labor leaders rose and fell. And so did radical "armies of liberation" led by folk-hero bandits, such as Pancho Villa and Emiliano Zapata, who looted churches and haciendas. In bloody skirmishes the outlaw armies fought the *federales*, or government troops, sent by a succession of short-term presidents. But those who suffered most were the poor. The Mexican populace was set upon by both the revolutionaries and the federal troops. They lost not only their homes and their meager possessions but their very lives. It is estimated that more than one million Mexicans were killed in the prolonged conflict.

Pedro Martínez, a Mexican villager, recalled the early years of the Revolution of 1910.

It reached the point where martial law was declared. There was no way of getting out now. At the end of 1913, and into 1914, you couldn't even step out of the village because if the government came and found you walking, they killed you.

The first village to be burned was Santa Maria, in 1913. . . .

Brigades of women and girls joined the fight during the Mexican Revolution. But failing to resist the advance of federal troops and outlaw armies, many citizens chose to migrate north.

It was entirely destroyed. The [soldiers] had burned everything. The dead were hanging from the trees. It was a massacre! Cows, oxen, pigs, and dogs had been killed and the people, poor things, went about picking up rotten meat to eat. All the corn and beans were burned. It was a terrible pity.

40

Not surprisingly, a great migration was soon under way. During the 1880s, while Porfirio Díaz was still in power, a relatively small number of Mexicans had started moving north across the border to work on railroads such as the Southern Pacific and the Santa Fe. This was especially true after the Chinese Exclusion Act of 1882 cut off the immigration of Asian rail workers into the United States.

Beginning in 1910, and continuing for the next twenty years, the trickle of immigrants northward became a steady stream, not just from Mexico's border regions but from the heart of the country. The means of transportation for many of the desperate travelers would be the railroads that Porfirio Díaz had built to bring Mexico wealth and stability. Some of the refugees were lucky enough to ride in the coaches. But others, dispossessed by the warring armies, had to perch precariously on the roofs of the moving cars. The scenes they viewed en route revealed ravaged lands, burned villages, and the hanged bodies of victims of the ongoing slaughter.

Mexican laborers were recruited for copper mining in Arizona in the early 1900s.

Three

The Great Migration

FLEEING VIOLENCE AND TERROR, POVERTY AND HOPELESSNESS, THE refugees of the Mexican Revolution of 1910 began arriving in the United States in numbers that would double its Mexican population twice in the next twenty years. Thus 250,000 Mexican residents in 1910 became 500,000 in 1920 and close to one million by 1930.

What jobs were there for these hundreds of thousands of newcomers trying to gain a foothold, primarily in the American Southwest? They would work as farmhands, miners, and as railroaders building and maintaining the miles of tracks stretching into once remote places. But where would they live and how? Their would-be employers had already established a pattern of offering the Mexican labor pool wages, working conditions, and living arrangements that were notoriously substandard. So the newcomers would live as close as possible to their employment and with the most minimal human comforts.

Soon families of agricultural laborers, including young children and the elderly, were picking sugar beets and cotton in Texas; vegetables, citrus fruits, and grapes in California; and apples and cherries as far north as Oregon and Washington. Having recently migrated from Mexico, these families now became migrant farmworkers in the United States, traveling north each summer and fall following the ripening harvests. Their homes would be labor camps made up of flimsy tents or rough wooden shacks, one room to a family, without electricity, sanitation, or running water. Nor were there any bathroom facilities in the fields where the migrant families labored for twelve to fourteen hours a day.

The camps provided no schooling, nor were there any child labor laws that prohibited the young from working as fruit and vegetable pickers. Once the growing season was over, the family might settle in a ramshackle dwelling in a barrio, or Mexican quarter, of one of the larger cities where the father and older boys would seek day labor in construction or other manual trades. The younger children might get in a bit of schooling, while the women of the family worked as domestics or peddled food or handicrafts. Chickens and goats were often kept by barrio families. But no matter how hard they struggled to get ahead, the cycle of poverty continually renewed itself.

Mexicans working in railroading or mining were often men on their own, trying to earn money to send back to their families in Mexico. Railroaders, whether alone or with their families, lived in boxcars or in shanties along the tracks, and were forced to purchase their food at a store run by the railroad company. Lucia Martínez described the experiences of her family in 1916:

My sixteen-year-old brother, who worked on the railroad tracks, only received twenty-five cents [at a time]. The bosses kept a list of what people bought to eat. When a check came, they gave us no

In Texas, refugees from Mexico found work in the cotton fields.

money because they said it had all gone for food. We only had potatoes, beans, flour, coffee, and sugar.

One day the commissary agent got mad at my older brother and said he was going to kill him. "We can't stay here any longer," my father announced. "Any day that man might attack Elidoro. Let's leave."

We didn't have a cent. Absolutely nothing. We left at one in the morning so no one would see us. We packed some suitcases with bedclothes and a little clothing. My mother fixed some biscuits and beans. . . . We walked along the track for 18 miles until we came to another town. At five in the afternoon we arrived. Some Mexicans who lived in houses made of railroad ties let us stay outside.

Yet, no matter how harsh their treatment, no matter how miserable their living and working conditions, Mexicans continued to be "pushed" out of their homeland because life was so intolerable. Mexican immigration would be affected far into the future, in fact, whenever a "push" came about as a result of economic need or political instability. It would also be influenced whenever a "pull" developed due to the demand for certain kinds of labor in the United States. The Chinese Exclusion Act of 1882 had created a "pull." With the banning of the "yellow peril" immigrants, many of whom had worked on the railroads, Mexican laborers were substituted. And so they took over the often backbreaking work of driving spikes, clearing the rails of rock slides and fallen trees, and reclaiming the tracks from flooded rivers and streams.

The entry of the United States into World War I in 1917 created another "pull" for Mexican labor. Still devastated by the ravages of the Mexican Revolution, Mexicans crossed the border in ever-increasing numbers. With American forces engaged in fighting abroad and factories gearing up for wartime production, new opportunities opened up that

Many who had fled the chaos and poverty of revolutionary Mexico found work laying rail lines.

took some Mexicans far beyond the drudgery of field labor and railroad maintenance.

Mexican workers, especially those who had immigrated in the earlier waves, began to find industrial jobs in the upper Midwest—in the meatpacking plants of Chicago, in the auto factories of Detroit, and in steel mills, paper factories, and chemical plants, as skilled machinists and mechanics. As a result, new communities of Mexicans formed in these northern cities, far from the border.

As long as the economy soared and there was no lack of jobs, the United States maintained very informal immigration policies toward Mexico. The two-thousand-mile boundary that separated the two nations was patrolled by a mere seventy-five border guards on horseback.

47

The U.S. Border Patrol was supposed to assess the literacy, health, and moral character of Mexican immigrants. But well into the 1920s, such entry requirements were largely overlooked.

Starting in 1917 Mexican immigrants were supposed to pass a literacy test, to be in good mental and physical health, and of good moral character. But few of these tests were ever administered.

By the time World War I ended in 1919, Mexican immigrants had begun to spread out beyond the Southwest, to become increasingly diverse in their job skills, and to establish communities that still maintained strong ties with their families and institutions back in Mexico.

IN SPITE OF THE LARGE NUMBER OF BORDER CROSSINGS THROUGHOUT the 1910s and 1920s, Mexicans made up only a fraction of the millions of immigrants that had been pouring into the United States since the

1880s. Most of these immigrants were from eastern and southern Europe—Jews, Italians, Poles, Czechs, Hungarians, and Balkan peoples. The end of World War I saw the return of America's soldiers, a reduction in industrial output, and too many European newcomers with limited skills chasing too few jobs.

The U.S. government's reaction to this problem was swift. In 1921 and again in 1924 it passed quota laws aimed at dramatically cutting back on unwanted European immigrants. Yet no quotas were set for Mexican immigration. And while the wartime jobs became less plentiful, there was always a need for farm labor and for cannery and construction workers on the West Coast. Even the Alaskan fisheries beckoned to the growing Mexican labor pool.

Meanwhile, the barrios of large cities, such as East Los Angeles, expanded into sprawling neighborhoods where Mexican tradespeople offered traditional foods, household goods, clothing, festival attire, and religious articles. Even though some barrio dwellers came and went, took up migrant labor or a distant job, or even returned to Mexico for a brief or prolonged stay, the barrio represented a corner of Mexico transplanted to the United States.

Barrio homes were made of adobe brick, stones, wooden planks, tin, or whatever construction materials came to hand, and were usually put together by a group of helpful neighbors. Amenities such as running water, sewer systems, and roads were makeshift at best, for the municipal authorities seldom extended such services into the Mexican quarters. Nonetheless, a rich cultural life sprang up, mirroring that of Mexico itself. Rooted in Native American tradition, Spanish Catholicism, and Mexican history, this hybrid culture unified and strengthened the community.

OUTSIDE THE BARRIO, HOWEVER, PREJUDICE WAS EVERYWHERE. IN PUBLIC places, Mexicans had to use separate bathrooms and drinking fountains. Anglo barbershops and eateries refused to serve them or at best permitted them to occupy a non-Anglo section of the facility. The same was true for swimming pools, movie theaters, and even places of worship. In Chicago, Roman Catholics refused to allow Mexicans into their churches.

Scorn came too from labor organizations that believed that workers who were used to higher wages couldn't compete for jobs with the poorly paid Mexicans. Yet many employers preferred Mexican workers for their docile acceptance of the wages and conditions offered to them.

Not all Mexicans who relocated to the United States submitted to the insults that were heaped upon them. Young people, especially male adolescents, were openly resentful of being called greasers or wetbacks, a slur implying they had entered the country by swimming across the Rio Grande. Barrio youths banded together to form clubs or gangs. The gangs were not necessarily intent on doing harm. Their original purpose was to help the youths defend their dignity and assert their *machismo*, or maleness. But matters did sometimes get out of hand.

Adults in the barrio population came together to establish *mutualistas*, or self-help societies. Their purpose was to assist newcomers to the community, offer migrant workers a temporary home, sponsor cultural events that reflected the barrio's Mexican heritage, apply to city authorities for much-needed public services, and provide funds for members in dire need. But the *mutualista* was a long way from becoming a political organization with enough power to improve significantly the lives of the Mexican minority.

Although political conditions in Mexico began to stabilize in the early 1930s, few Mexican Americans thought of returning permanently to their homeland. In fact, the news from north of the border, with all its difficulties, was economically encouraging to Mexicans. And substantial immigration might have continued indefinitely were it not for the onset of the Great Depression, which struck the United States beginning in 1930.

The causes of the depression were manifold—overproduction of manufactured goods and farm products, high prices, low wages, too much buying on credit, and a wildly inflated stock market that collapsed on October 29, 1929. Almost overnight millions of people lost their jobs, businesses closed, banks failed, and Americans began to experience poverty and homelessness such as they had never known before.

A widespread fear of a continuing influx of Mexican immigrants was felt throughout the nation. With jobless Americans ready to take any work they could find, nobody wanted new laborers arriving from south of the border. Verbal attacks on Mexicans became fierce and ugly. They were, according to public figures, "racial inferiors," "mongrels," and a "threat to the population." Even the venerable *New York Times* printed an editorial on May 16, 1930, that stated, "It is folly to pretend that the more recently arrived Mexicans, who are largely of Indian blood, can be absorbed and incorporated into the American race."

But, as it turned out, it was not only new arrivals from Mexico who were unwelcome. Mexican Americans who had established themselves and their families in the United States, had jobs there and businesses, had become citizens or who had even been born there, were about to become an army of deportees.

Deported Mexicans try to put a cheerful face on the loss of their jobs and homes in the United States.

Four

Braceros and Deportees

"Mexicans, go home!"

This was the rallying cry of newspaper editorials, politicians, and labor unions. As the rapid effects of the Great Depression of the 1930s began to be felt, Mexicans received much of the blame for joblessness in rural areas, small towns, and big cities. All Mexicans, whether they were recent arrivals or had lived in the Southwest most of their lives, whether legal residents of the United States or not, were subject to roundups by local police or government agents, and faced with possible deportation to Mexico.

California and Texas were particularly brutal in their disregard for the civil rights of documented Mexican Americans. Whether forcibly ejected or persuaded to leave "voluntarily," numerous inhabitants of the barrios of Los Angeles packed whatever they could carry and were put onto trains. The deportation authorities paid their fare of about fifteen dollars apiece directly to the railroad in advance. Texas, with the largest

Mexican population at the time, deported more than 100,000 Mexicans during the early 1930s.

As the depression deepened, poor Anglo transients appeared who were willing to accept the dwindling number of menial, drudge jobs—on the ranches and farms, on the railroads, and in the factories—that had once been held by Mexicans. The same was true for jobs in the cotton fields and copper mines of Arizona. As a result, Mexicans were loaded onto trucks and driven across the border. A notorious case in Arizona was that of a woman named Carmen Calderón. Although four of her six children were citizens, having been born in the United States, her entire family was shipped back to Mexico in 1936.

Jorge Acevedo, who was living in Maravilla, an East Los Angeles barrio, described its inhabitants, even U.S. citizens, being ordered to leave by truck early one morning.

Families were not asked what they would like to take along, or told what they needed . . . or even where they were going. "Get in the truck." . . . Families were separated. . . . They pushed most of my family in one van, and somehow in all the shouting and pushing I was separated and got stuck in another van. It was a very big one with boards across it for us to sit on. Nobody knew what was happening or where we were going. Someone said, to a health station.

We drove all day. The driver wouldn't stop for bathroom nor food nor water. The driver was drinking and became happier as he went along. . . . It was dark when he finally ran the truck off the road. Everyone knew by now that we had been deported. Nobody knew why, but there was a lot of hatred and anger.

During *La Crisis*, as Mexican Americans called the Great Depression, many who remained in the Southwest fought off hunger by gathering wild greens, cactus fruit, and the pods of the spiny mesquite tree, which were

A truckload of Mexicans from Houston, Texas, are about to be returned to their country of origin during the Great Depression of the 1930s.

usually fed to cattle. At worst they picked through the garbage dumps.

In Crystal City, Texas, not far from the border, one Mexican-American community held on by working in the spinach fields. The barrio of this south Texas town consisted of frame shacks of one or two rooms with dirt floors and tin roofs. Windows lacking panes of glass were covered with flour sacks. Cooking was done outdoors over an open fire. A single outdoor water faucet served several families, and flies buzzed around the open toilets. Diarrhea and tuberculosis were rampant. Children who did attend school seldom got beyond third or fourth grade.

Some Mexican laborers survived the lean years by working in the Texas spinach fields and living in shacks in a makeshift barrio.

Repatriation was the polite term for the deportation of half a million Mexican Americans during the 1930s. In 1932 alone, some 200,000 were forced to leave. The Mexican government could do little for the trainloads and busfuls of arrivals and had to put some into refugee camps. For Mexicans who had been longtime residents of the United States, it was often hard to adjust to life in Mexico. Their Mexican neighbors referred to them as gringos, the disparaging term for a foreigner. As a result, the deportees felt they belonged nowhere.

New Mexico was the only southwestern state that did not aggressively pursue the deportation of its Mexican residents. Its large Spanish *criollo* population had already established a strong political base in the state. In 1928, its former governor, Octaviano A. Larrazolo, was appointed to the U.S. Senate to complete the term of a deceased senator. And, in 1936, Dennis Chávez became the first Hispanic to be elected to the U.S. Senate. A Democrat under President Franklin Roosevelt, Chávez fought for equal rights for Latinos until his death in 1962.

MOST HISTORIANS AGREE THAT, WHILE THE 1930s NEW DEAL PROGRAMS of President Roosevelt attempted to address some of the worst agonies of the depression, such as hunger and homelessness, it was World War II that put the United States back on the road to full employment. Once again, in 1942, as at the start of U.S. participation in World War I in 1917, the country had so great a need for armed-forces personnel and for workers in war-related industries that a labor shortage developed.

As before, Mexican labor was in high demand, especially for field work and railroad building and maintenance. This time, however, a formal arrangement was entered into by the governments of Mexico and the United States. It was known as the Bracero Program. Its very name *bracero*, meaning day laborer, comes from the Spanish word *brazo*, or arm.

As Mexico, for once, was in a position to dictate the terms it made every attempt to ensure fair treatment for its people. Recruitment of

Mexican women were among those recruited for railroad work, in an attempt to remedy the labor shortage created by World War II.

braceros was to be based on written labor contracts of specified lengths, approved and overseen by both governments. There were to be no *enganchadores*, freelance, often untrustworthy, labor recruiters. The American employer or the U.S. government was to pay transportation to the work site. The Mexican government stated its hope that there would be far less racial discrimination against Mexican workers in American eateries, in public facilities, on buses, or in short everywhere. The state of Texas, because of its many abuses of Mexicans in the past, was to receive no *braceros* at all.

The Bracero Program lasted throughout World War II, a period during which the U.S. government's shameful internment of Japanese Americans robbed the nation of many of its skilled agriculturalists. After the war ended in 1945, the Bracero Program was renewed several times, so that it spanned twenty-two years, from 1942 to 1964. During that period, nearly five million contracts were issued for temporary Mexican farm and railroad workers.

As might have been expected, however, the "pull" of jobs in the United States stimulated the inflow of many Mexican illegals who were unable to qualify for the Bracero Program. Texas, since it had been denied *braceros*, was a particular magnet for the so-called wetbacks during the war years and afterward. Even though Texas appointed a Good Neighbor Commission and finally was permitted to receive *braceros* in 1947, there was no stopping the influx of the undocumented.

By the early 1950s, it was estimated that close to one million illegals were attempting to cross the border annually. With the economy no longer on a wartime footing, many groups were openly critical of both the *braceros* and the illegal immigrants. Labor unions felt that the non-resident Mexican labor force lowered agricultural wages, thereby cutting out the American worker.

In addition, Mexican-American groups that were well-established in the United States wanted to see an end to so much Mexican immigration.

Los Braceros—The Migratory Workers

The *corrido* is a traditional Mexican folk ballad that can be spoken or sung. This song is a lament for the life of the *bracero*, the migrant laborer who, despite his hard work, may find himself cheated of his wages and even deported.

Ya son mu - chos los pai - sa - nos_____ que se
Man - y of my coun - try - men now_____ at the

van al_____ ex - tran - je - ro,_____
bor - der_____ are all lined up,_____

Y pa - ra po - der sa - lir,_____ se con -
And to be a - ble to cross it,_____ as *bra* -

tra - tan_____ de "bra - ce - ros."_____
*ce - ros*_____ they have signed up._____

Des - pués de lar - gos seis me - ses_____ les re -
Af - ter six months have gone by and_____ when the

co - gen_____ los pa - pe - les,_____
beets have_____ all been crat - ed,_____

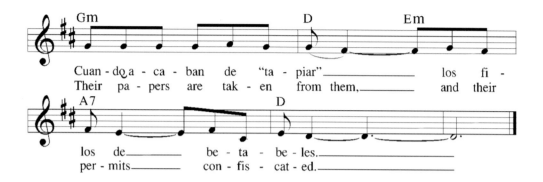

Cuan - do a - ca - ban   de   "ta - piar"_____   los   fi -
Their   pa - pers   are   tak - en   from them,_____   and   their

los   de_____   be - ta - be - les._____
per - mits_____   con - fis - cat - ed._____

Se desiertan de los campos
Y se hacen los inocentes,
Se van buscando trabajo
Durmiendo bajo las puentes.
Y después de tantas penas
Si es que ellos tuvieron suerte,
Caminan por los desiertos
Enfrentándose a la muerte.

Se los llevan los rancheros
A la pizca de algodón.
Para no pargarles nada
Les echan la inmigración.
De ahí van a las prisiones
Y graves penas les dan,
Luego los mandan pelones
Al puerto de Mazatlán.

Cuentan cien mil mexicanos
Los que no están inmigrados,
Entre ellos hay desertores,
"Alambristas" y "mojados."
Y a con esta me despido
Y los vuelvo a amonestar;
Que no salgan del terruño
Que despues les va a pesar.

Leaving the bare fields behind them,
For employment they go seeking.
Hoping the police don't find them,
Under bridges they are sleeping,
And after all of their sorrows,
If they're lucky and not hunted,
They travel over the deserts,
Where by death they are confronted.

Then they are taken by ranchers
To pick cotton on plantations.
Then in order not to pay them,
They call up the Immigration.
Now they have nothing but trouble,
As to prison they're transported.
Then with their heads freshly shaven,
To Mazatlán they're deported.

A hundred thousand *mexicanos*
Tell those who've not immigrated,
And who have passed through the fences,
And as wetbacks, who have waded—
With this I will now say so long,
And remember that I said it:
Don't ever part from your country—
If you do, you will regret it.

Among them was the League of United Latin American Citizens (LULAC), established in 1929. Another critic was the Mexican-American leader, George I. Sánchez of the University of Texas. Quoted in the *New York Times* on March 27, 1951, under the heading "Peons in West Lowering Culture," Sánchez said:

> From a cultural standpoint, the influx of a million or more wetbacks a year transforms the Spanish-speaking people of the Southwest from an ethnic group that might be assimilated with reasonable facility into what I call a culturally indigestible peninsula of Mexico.

Mexican Americans also felt that the "wetback crisis" was pushing wages down for American citizens of Mexican origin. As in the case of many immigrant groups, those who had arrived earlier were not always welcoming of their later-arriving countrymen and -women. The general public, too, was inflamed with anti-wetback feeling. The illegals were accused of causing disease, labor unrest, immorality, and crime. Employers in the Southwest, the Pacific Northwest, and the Midwest were threatened with severe penalties if found to be harboring illegal workers.

As a result, in June 1954, the Immigration and Naturalization Service (INS) was empowered to launch "Operation Wetback," another massive repatriation program designed to deport illegal immigrants not just across the border, but this time deep into Mexico.

To accomplish this purpose, trains, buses, aircraft, and boats were employed. When the program ended four years later, in 1958, the INS claimed to have deported three to four million illegal Mexican immigrants.

Once more in the 1950s, as during the height of the Great Depression, the United States abruptly withdrew the welcome mat for

These Mexicans waiting outside a relief office were among those who sought public assistance when jobs became less plentiful after the close of World War II.

The zoot suit of the 1940s was popular with youths everywhere. Note the long key chain, which was an important feature of the outfit.

Mexican laborers once they were no longer needed in such great numbers. But despite this pattern of less stringent immigration policies followed by mass deportations, the needy would continue to risk the journey north as long as the United States offered the slightest hope of economic betterment.

ONE MAJOR INSTANCE OF ANTI-MEXICAN FEELING DURING THE WAR YEARS in the United States was a series of events known as the Zoot Suit Riots. These disturbances took place in 1942 and 1943, while the Bracero

Program was in full swing and about 400,000 Mexican Americans were serving in the U.S. armed forces.

Like most American youth in the 1940s, under-eighteen males in the Los Angeles barrios had taken to wearing the "zoot suit" of the jitter-buggers—couples who performed the popular energetic dance of the day. The zoot suit featured an oversized jacket with broad shoulders, high-waisted baggy pants that tapered sharply at the ankle, and a flat, broad-brimmed fedora hat. Being in fashion was an attempt to assimilate on the part of these mainly second-generation Mexican Americans. For the Los Angeles youths felt the stigma of discrimination common to their people. Unwelcome in many restaurants, movie theaters, and most other public places, they asserted their teenaged machismo by clustering in gangs.

On the morning of August 2, 1942, a dying youth, José Díaz, was found near a pond called the Sleepy Lagoon where the local gang members often went to swim and sometimes to rumble, or fight.

Although an autopsy failed to reveal the exact cause of Díaz's death, the newspapers and the law frightened the public with implications that a "Boy Gang Terror Wave" was on the loose. Twenty-two members of a gang known as the 38th Street Club were arrested and made to stand trial for conspiracy to murder. They were not allowed to clean themselves up, thus appearing before the court dirty and disheveled and in their zoot suits, which were seen as a symbol of rebellion and disrespect. Seventeen of the defendants were convicted—twelve of murder and five of assault.

An appeals court was to overturn the conviction in October 1944, stating that there was a lack of evidence connecting the seventeen youths to Díaz's death and that, furthermore, their constitutional rights had been violated. But in the year following the Sleepy Lagoon case, the press so inflamed the public that there were frequent clashes between the youths and the police, based on the assumption that all zoot suiters were not only gang members but potential criminals.

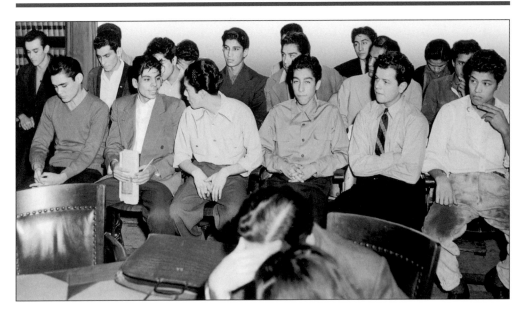

Members of the 38th Street Club, accused of the murder of another Mexican teenager, were arrested and tried in the notorious Sleepy Lagoon case.

As a result, on the nights of June 4, 5, and 6, 1943, a race riot broke out in Los Angeles. More than two hundred Anglo soldiers and sailors invaded the barrio and began beating up Mexican youths. Those in zoot suits were stripped as well as bloodied.

On June 7, Anglo servicemen, joined by civilians, took their racial fury to downtown Los Angeles, targeting Mexicans as well as Filipinos and blacks in movie theaters, eateries, and bars. The Los Angeles police made little attempt to stop these attacks, and the military police were eventually called in to restore order.

But the race riots of that summer were far from over. Los Angeles was followed by Chicago, Philadelphia, and Detroit. The Detroit riots were so severe that they resulted in the deaths of twenty-five blacks and nine whites.

It was ironic that the United States should have been ripped apart by racial hatred at the same time as its soldiers from all ethnic backgrounds

Anglo soldiers and sailors armed with clubs beat Mexican youths in Los Angeles during the zoot suit riots of June 1943.

were fighting its enemies in the Pacific Ocean, the Aleutian Islands, Europe, North Africa, and in the China-Burma-India theater.

Mexican Americans served, in fact, in a number that was disproportionately high in relation to their total population—nearly half a million out of 2.7 million people. And they also made up a higher percentage of combat divisions, such as the marines and the paratroopers, than any other ethnic group.

There are several reasons why Mexican Americans had such a strong presence in the armed forces. Young men who were Mexican nationals living in the United States joined because the military offered easy access to U.S. citizenship by shortening the waiting period. Few, even those who were citizens, had jobs that qualified them for deferment, and they felt that serving their country would result in a better public image and thus better work opportunities and fairer treatment at home.

Among the most historic Mexican-American fighters in World War II were the members of the New Mexico National Guard, which had been transferred to the Philippines and were subsequently called upon to defend the Bataan Peninsula.

Despite stubborn American resistance, the Philippines fell to Japan early in 1942. On the infamous Bataan Death March 42,000 starving and exhausted American prisoners were made to walk 70 miles to prison camps. More than half died. One-fourth of the men on the Bataan Death March were Mexican Americans.

At the close of World War II, Mexicans received scores of medals, such as the Silver Star, Bronze Star, Distinguished Service Cross, and Purple Heart, as a result of their heroism abroad. And twelve servicemen of Mexican descent received the highest of all military awards given in the United States—the Congressional Medal of Honor.

Yet, decorated or not, uniformed Mexican-American veterans continued to be refused service in establishments that habitually did not serve Mexicans. And in Three Rivers, Texas, a local funeral chapel refused to

Although many received military honors, of the nearly 500,000 Mexican Americans who served in World War II, a large percentage were casualties.

perform a burial service for Félix Longoria, a heroic soldier whose body had been returned home from the Philippines for interment. So outraged was the Mexican community of south Texas that—with the support of Senator Lyndon Johnson—Longoria's body was subsequently laid to rest in Arlington National Cemetery.

Chicano power became the rallying cry of younger Mexican Americans in the decades following World War II.

Five

Chicano Power

WORLD WAR II PROVED TO BE A TURNING POINT FOR MINORITY AND oppressed peoples living in the United States. It was inevitable that returning Mexican-American veterans who had distinguished themselves in battle, won commissions, and even commanded Anglo troops, should refuse to suffer the humiliations of the past.

Other groups, too, were making demands in the postwar era. The black civil rights struggle became an urgent issue. The feminist movement sprang up to protest the social, financial, and political status of women. And the youth of America expressed its alienation, rebelling against everything from the social mores of the past to the Vietnam War. So it hardly came as a surprise that the country's Latino population should have raised its voice in a strong, new bid for cultural recognition and political power.

It did so under the banner of the name "Chicano," which is derived from *Mexicano*. Before the 1960s, Chicano was often used as slang to disparage lower-class Mexicans. But like the African-American preference for the word *black*, the name Chicano was newly equated with pride and activism.

Most of the Chicano activists of the 1960s were at least second-generation Mexican Americans. They were better educated and more Americanized than their parents and had more familiarity with the nation's Mexican communities. Some had been the zoot suiters of the 1940s, too young to fight in World War II, while others were the veterans of that conflict.

Established Hispanic rights organizations such as LULAC had long been fighting for an end to bias and for equal education and employment opportunities. Directly after the war, in 1948, Latinos had founded the American GI Forum to help veterans obtain their GI Bill rights with regard to housing and education. The Forum soon expanded its goals to include voter registration and to advocate a host of social and political reforms. Both LULAC and the American GI Forum were started in Texas. The American GI Forum was organized in direct response to the refusal of burial service for Félix Longoria in Three Rivers. Both organizations had developed local chapters in many other states.

But the Chicano movement saw the need for a stronger advocacy based on the historical unity of La Raza, "the race." One of its pioneers was Rodolfo "Corky" Gonzales. Born to migrant sugar beet workers in Denver, Colorado, in 1928, Gonzales had a varied career as a boxer, auto insurance agent, and poet and playwright. His "Spiritual Plan of Aztlán" was devised to provide the Chicano people with a symbolic territorial base. It was rooted in the belief that once, centuries before the Anglos took the land, there had existed in the southwestern United States a "northern" kingdom called Aztlán. The plan was adopted at the National Chicano Liberation Youth Conference held in Denver in March 1969.

The early years of the Chicano movement were the most radical.

Identifying themselves as a "bronze people" steeped in their own "bronze culture," the activists advocated the rejection of all things American. They saw separatism rather than assimilation as their best course, and demanded local control of schools, civic and business affairs, political offices, and even banks in their own communities. Part of the inspiration for what might be called the "roots versus integration" approach was found in Gonzales's epic poem "Yo Soy Joaquín" ("I Am Joaquín"), which encouraged its readers to proudly embrace their heritage. The title is taken from the Mexican California outlaw, Joaquín Murieta, who went on a rampage in the 1850s after Anglos robbed him of his claim to the gold mine he had been working and also killed his brother. The poem, however, reaches beyond the plight of Murieta and embraces all of Mexican and Mexican-American history, which is seen as one of exploitation and oppression. It contains the following lines:

> I am Joaquín
> in a country that has wiped out
> all my history,
> and stifled my pride. . . .
> My knees are caked with mud.
> My hands are calloused from the hoe.
> I have made the Anglo rich. . . .
> Here I stand
> poor in money
> arrogant in pride.

The Chicano agenda included demands for bilingual education and for a school curriculum that included the history of La Raza and of the Chicano power struggle. The late 1960s saw Mexican-American students walk out of classes in Texas, Colorado, and New Mexico. In the spring of 1968, 10,000 young Chicanos marched out of the high schools of East

Rodolfo "Corky" Gonzales, Denver's popular rights activist, was among the more radical Chicano leaders.

Los Angeles clamoring for multicultural education, schools with better facilities, and more Latino teachers and administrators.

East Los Angeles was also the birthplace of the Brown Berets. This paramilitary group modeled itself on the African-American group, the Black Panthers, and the Young Lords of the mainland Puerto Ricans.

A climactic event in Los Angeles was the anti-Vietnam rally of August 29, 1970. As in World War II, a disproportionate number of Mexican Americans were fighting in the Vietnam War and were suffering an exceptionally high casualty rate. The Chicano movement opposed the war and wanted peace without delay. On the day of the protest, twenty to thirty thousand marchers turned out, as did hundreds of police officers.

Women as well as men joined the opposition group known as the Brown Berets.

The crowd, already incensed by past instances of police brutality, became unruly. In the melee that followed, the police fired into the crowd. Many were wounded, more than two hundred were arrested, and three died. Stunned, the protesters learned that one of the victims was Rubén Salazar, the reporter for the *Los Angeles Times* who had been the voice of the Mexican-American community on the newspaper.

Only six months earlier, on February 6, 1970, the Mexican-born Salazar had written a column for the *Times* in which he had tried to explain the angst of the Chicano activists to both Hispanic and Anglo readers.

A Chicano is a Mexican American with a non-Anglo image of himself. He resents being told Columbus "discovered" America when the Chicano's ancestors, the Mayans and the Aztecs, founded highly sophisticated civilizations centuries before Spain financed the Italian explorer's trip to the "New World."

Chicanos resent also Anglo pronouncements that Chicanos are "culturally deprived" or that the fact that they speak Spanish is a "problem." Chicanos will tell you that their culture predates that of the Pilgrims and that Spanish was spoken in America before English and so the "problem" is not theirs but the Anglos' who don't speak Spanish. . . .

Mexican Americans, the second largest minority in the country and the largest in the Southwestern states . . . have always had difficulty making up their minds what to call themselves. In New Mexico they call themselves Spanish-Americans. In other parts of the Southwest they call themselves Americans of Mexican descent, people with Spanish surnames or Hispanos. Why, ask some Mexican-Americans, can't we just call ourselves Americans?

Chicanos are trying to explain why not. Mexican-Americans, though indigenous to the Southwest, are on the lowest rung scholastically, economically, socially, and politically. Chicanos feel cheated. They want to effect change. Now. . . . That is why Mexican-American activists flaunt the barrio word Chicano—as an act of defiance and a badge of honor.

LIKE ALL PROTEST MOVEMENTS, THE BID FOR CHICANO POWER RESULTED in both gains and losses. In 1968 Congress passed the Bilingual Education Act. The act provided federal aid to public schools that undertook to teach immigrant children in their own language, mainly in the early grades. And an amendment to the act in 1974 added a provision to encourage multicultural education so that immigrant youth could learn about its heritage.

On the other hand, numerous objections arose to bilingual education, and the argument rages to the present day. Opponents even included a number of Latino leaders who felt the only route to real educational advancement was total immersion in English from the earliest grades. As a result, a rash of reversals came about in the 1980s when several states, including California and Arizona, passed laws declaring English their "official" language.

The Chicano power movement of the 1960s also saw mixed results in its efforts to reform U.S. immigration policies. On the negative side, Chicanismo spurred the passage of the 1965 Immigration and Nationality Act, which limited new arrivals from the Western Hemisphere to 120,000 annually. This act was followed by a 1976 ruling, which placed a ceiling of 20,000 per year from any one country in the Americas. At the same time, the Chicano pride movement drew Mexicans north across the border. In spite of a vastly enlarged U.S. Border Patrol using sophisticated means of detection—helicopters, radar, and infrared and electronic sensors—nothing was to stem the flow of illegal aliens in their desperate search for economic betterment.

DURING THE 1960s, AS THE LEADERS OF THE CHICANO MOVEMENT WERE urging cultural identification and political self-rule, another leader arose who was to concern himself with the economic plight of his people.

His name was César Chávez, and no one could have known more than he about the lives of the migrant workers of the Southwest. Chávez was born in Yuma, Arizona, in 1927. During the Great Depression of the 1930s, his family lost the farm that his grandfather had homesteaded in the 1880s. Although homeless, the Chávez family managed to avoid the mass deportations to Mexico by turning to migrant labor.

At the age of ten, Chávez was a child agricultural worker in the fields

Mexicans attempting to enter the United States illegally are stopped by the Border Patrol. Stricter immigration policies were one result of the Chicano power movement.

and vineyards of California. In summer he picked beans, chili peppers, and corn; in early autumn, grapes and prunes. Late autumn found the Chávez family in the cotton fields, and winter found them gathering crops of cabbage, lettuce, and broccoli. Traveling around so much,

César Chávez vastly improved the often wretched working and living conditions of California's migrant workers.

Chávez attended thirty different schools in short stints and was never able to complete eighth grade. Nor did he ever forget the humiliation of trying once to order a hamburger in a California diner that refused to serve nonwhites. He had been called a "damned dumb Mexican" and was laughed out of the place with tears welling in his eyes.

With the outbreak of World War II, Chávez joined the navy.

Afterward he settled in the San Jose, California, barrio known ironically as Sal Si Puedes, "Get out If You Can." During the postwar years he had begun studying the unionization of factory workers and wondered if a union could be formed for the benefit of migrant farmworkers.

In 1962, Chávez started driving around from one migrant camp to another, focusing on the grape-growing region of California in and around the town of Delano. His goal in organizing the grape pickers was to establish a minimum wage, attain safer working conditions with regard to the use of pesticides, provide toilets and drinking water in the vineyards, and secure better living conditions and on-site schooling for the children of migrant workers.

When the powerful grape growers refused to negotiate, Chávez took the bold step of calling a strike and instituting a nationwide table-grape boycott. *La huelga*, the strike, for Chávez's *La Causa* was to last five years, from 1965 to 1970. Although the grape pickers were turned out of their campsites, Chávez's union, the National Farm Workers Association, became affiliated with the AFL-CIO, the nation's foremost trade and industrial union, which helped sustain the strikers until some of the smaller growers settled. *La Causa* was also supported by important national political figures such as Robert Kennedy and by consumer groups all over the country who refused to buy nonunion grapes. Likewise, unionized shippers and dockworkers refused to handle any grape cartons that did not bear the UFW symbol, a black Aztec eagle.

César Chávez's struggle to unionize California's migrant workers included women organizers as well as men. Jessie Lopez De La Cruz explains how she, the daughter of a migrant family, became active in the National Farm Workers' union.

Growing up, I could see all the injustices and I would think, "If only I could do something about it! If only there was somebody who could do something about it!" That was always at the back of my mind. And after I was married, I cared about what was going on, but couldn't do anything. So I went to work and I came home to clean the house, and I fixed food for the next day, took care of the children and the next day went back to work. The whole thing over and over again. Politics to me was something foreign, something I didn't know about. . . .

But then late one night in 1962, there was a knock at the door and there were three men. One of them was César Chávez. And the next thing I knew, they were sitting around our table talking about a union . . . for the farmworkers. Arnold [my husband] was attending their meetings at Fresno, but I didn't. I'd either stay home or stay outside in the car. But then César said, "The women have to be involved. They're the ones working out in the fields with their husbands. If you can take the women out to the fields, you can certainly take them to meetings." So I sat up straight and said to myself, "*That's* what I want!"

During the strike years, Chávez led a 300-mile march to the state capital in Sacramento and endured a 25-day fast. His victory in establishing a successful union for migrant agricultural workers improved wages and living conditions not only in the vineyards but for other farmworkers, especially the lettuce pickers.

But the success of *La Causa* had a downside, too. During the strike years, some growers started using machines rather than people to harvest their crops. Others fought agricultural unionization by turning to the ever-present labor pool of Mexican illegals.

The workers that Chávez organized were all either legal residents or citizens of the United States, and he had long been a critic of illegal immigration. It was even rumored that in his early years of union organizing Chávez had gone so far as to report undocumented Mexican farmworkers.

By the 1970s, Chávez was in direct conflict with the leaders of the

Strikers were not only turned out of their campsites. In some cases, the powerful grape growers called in armed guards who maced the picketers.

Chicano movement. He saw unchecked immigration as the foe of the National Farm Workers' union because it supplied an unlimited number of strikebreakers who would in the long run "jeopardize the rights of all farmworkers." The Chicano organizations countered with the reminder that the illegals were, after all, the brothers and sisters of the oppressed workers for whom Chávez had fought. Was it fair that they should live in ravines or in cardboard or plywood shacks with plastic coverings and dirt floors? Was it right that they should sleep on junkyard mattresses and be without toilets, electricity, or drinking water; that they should have to cook on outdoor fires and survive on beans?

Long before his death in 1993, César Chávez changed his position on illegal immigration and came to terms with the Chicano point of view. One of his recommendations was an "amnesty for illegal aliens." He vowed that the NFW would "support their efforts to obtain legal documents and equal rights, including the right of collective bargaining."

The amnesty idea that Chávez advocated came about as the Immigration Reform and Control Act of 1986. The act was a partially successful attempt to give illegal aliens who had lived and worked in the United States since January 1, 1982 a chance to come forward and apply for legal residency, thereby obtaining the "green" card giving them permission to work. It was estimated that 3.9 million Mexican workers were eligible for legalization. Yet only 2 million applied. Fear of being found ineligible and of facing apprehension and deportation kept many from registering during the one-year signup period.

As the 1970s gave way to the 1980s, much of the militancy of the reform movement born in the 1960s showed signs of waning. César Chávez, the power behind the NFW and the migrant farmworkers' strike, began to accept the inevitable flow of illegal immigration and sought ways of accommodating it.

As for the Chicano movement, the defiant Rodolfo "Corky"

Members of the National Farm Workers' Association display their symbol, a black Aztec eagle, and the word huelga, *meaning strike, on their march to the state capital.*

Gonzales, who had once led his "Corky's Commandoes" on invasions of Denver school board meetings, finally lost support. At the same time, Latino leaders began to engage more readily in local political discourse with Anglos. And the younger generation of the 1980s, which had long ago discarded the myth of Aztlán, was—for better or worse—tending to embrace American culture and to seek its place within it.

A Border Patrol officer, using an infrared camera, scans the terrain between Mexico and the United States to detect the movement of illegal immigrants trying to cross in the night.

Six

The Uneasy Borderland

ON A MOONLESS NIGHT A GROUP OF FOUR MEN AND TWO WOMEN DRESSED in dark drab clothing lope forward in a semicrouched position, their attention fixed on their leader to whom each has paid a sum of several hundred dollars. Never taking their eyes off the figure in front of them, they try to step lightly and to stay close to the desert scrub thinking it might offer some cover should the infrared beams of a U.S. Border Patrol helicopter or ground vehicle pick them out in the dark.

La Migra, as the U.S.-Mexican border guards of the Immigration and Naturalization Service are known, are everywhere. Would-be Mexican illegals trying to enter the United States have been warned that even when you cannot see them, they can see you. For the INS has ground sensors that are so responsive they can detect the weight and the heat of a human body.

There are, of course, many places to cross along the 2,000-mile border

The tortilla curtain is the name given to this 14-mile stretch of welded steel fencing that divides Mexico from California.

between the two countries. The Rio Grande runs for 1,250 miles between Mexico and Texas. At shallow points it is possible to wade across the river, or it may be necessary to swim.

The rest of the border is mostly desert, blocked here and there by long fences. At its extreme western edge, the border is fortified with a

Wading across the shallows of the Rio Grande is one way those without the proper documents enter the United States.

10-foot-high, 14-mile-long welded steel fence known as the tortilla curtain. This fence separates the Mexican peninsula of Baja California, near Tijuana, from California and the interstate highway that leads to nearby San Diego and northward. Young Mexicans have learned to breach this fence and to search for cover in the canyons that lace the landscape in this coastal region.

Attempting to cross on one's own is risky no matter what the route. Many Mexicans use the services of a guide, a Mexican or an American, skilled in getting his or her group past the difficult terrain of the immediate border area under cover of darkness. Often, after a first night of hiding out, the newcomers are met by a prearranged car or van and conducted to a city such as Los Angeles or to an agricultural area where they will find work. Guides, who have been known to charge as much as $1,200 for a crossing, usually require a down payment and collect the rest from the immigrant's pay.

Those who specialize in smuggling Mexicans across the border are known as *coyotes*. Like the crafty animal, the *coyote* often turns out to be a shifty broker, or go-between, who acts on the sly. The clients who purchase the *coyotes'* services are the *pollos*, or chickens.

There are, of course, no guarantees that the smuggling operation will be successful. *Coyote*-led illegals have been caught in great numbers and returned to Mexico. Often a number of attempts are made by the same *pollo*, as described here by Miguel Torres, who in 1977 was caught three times:

I went to Tijuana. . . . There's a person there that will get in contact with you. They call him the Coyote. He walks around town, and if he sees someone wandering around alone, he says, "Hello, do you have relatives in the United States?" And if you say yes, he says he can arrange it through a friend. It costs $250 or $300.

The Coyote rounded up me and five other guys, and then he got in contact with a guide to take us across the border. We had to go through the hills and the desert, and we had to swim through a river. I was a little scared. Then we come to a highway and a man was there with a van, pretending to fix his motor. Our guide said hello, and the man jumped into the car and we ran and jumped in, too. He began to drive down the highway fast and we knew we were . . . in the United States. [But after two months Torres was caught and taken across the border to Mexicali.]

When we arrived in Mexicali, they let us go. We caught a bus to Tijuana, and then at Tijuana, that night, we found the Coyote again and we paid him and we came back the next day. I had to pay $250 again, but this time he knew me and he let me pay $30 then and $30 each week . . .

Altogether I've been caught three times this year and made the trip over here four times. It's cost me one thousand dollars but it's still better than what I was making in Mexico City.

There have also been frequent tragedies such as drownings in the Rio Grande, suffocations in sealed vans and trucks, and highway deaths. So many newly arrived Mexicans have been hit by speeding cars on Interstate 5 near San Diego that yellow warning signs have been posted showing running silhouettes of a man, a woman, and a child.

ALTHOUGH THE U.S.–MEXICAN BORDER REGION IS CHARACTERIZED BY long barren stretches of river and desert, it is far from uninhabited. "Twin cities," one on either side of the national boundary, mark it at intervals. Connected by a bridge or a road, cities such as Matamoros, Mexico, and Brownsville, Texas; Ciudad Juarez, Mexico, and El Paso, Texas; Nogales, Mexico, and Nogales, Arizona; and Tijuana, Mexico, and the San Diego area in California, carry on a lively trade in commerce, cultural affairs, and tourism.

Americans can cross these borders easily as long as they have valid documents for their return. Mexicans can enter the United States for shopping or family visits on a 72-hour pass, provided they do not travel more than 25 miles from their point of entry and do not seek work in the United States. Today, these visitors come in large numbers from deep inside Mexico via express trains that take them directly to the Mexican border cities.

There are also many Mexican commuters who live in a Mexican border

Mexican women at work in a maquiladora, *or foreign-owned assembly plant, on the Mexican side of the border*

city but cross every day to work on the U.S. side. They have regular jobs as hotel workers, landscapers, domestics, mechanics, and construction and factory workers.

A major feature of the Mexican side of the border has been its development as the site of a broad range of manufacturing activity through the Mexican-initiated Border Industrialization Program. The roots of the

BIP, as well as the Mexican commuter-worker program, go back to 1964 when the Bracero Program officially ended.

The BIP offers a free-trade zone to American and other foreign industry, including many Asian-owned corporations. Raw materials are shipped duty-free into Mexico for assembly and finishing by Mexican workers who are paid on a wage scale that is lower than in the United States but higher than average for Mexico. Today, these *maquiladoras*, or "runaway" shops, as the assembly plants are called, are Mexico's second-largest source of foreign exchange, with oil first and tourism third.

Staffed mainly by female workers, the *maquiladoras* produce textiles and apparel, auto parts, power tools, electronics, electrical items, optics, musical instruments, toys, and a host of other manufactured articles purchased by American consumers. One only has to read the words "Made in Mexico" on garments, dry goods, and name-brand appliances to assess the volume of products now being turned out by the several thousand *maquiladoras* that employ hundreds of thousands of workers. Tijuana alone manufactures so many television sets that it calls itself the television capital of the world.

But has this enterprise been truly beneficial for Mexico? American manufacturers with plants just south of the border feel that they are making a contribution to both economies. Mexican workers are paid a "reasonable" wage ($30 to $50 a week in the Tijuana television assembly plants), and American consumers are able to buy TVs and other items more cheaply than if they were made by workers in the United States receiving the minimum wage or more.

A look at the lives of the assembly-line workers themselves reveals a number of drawbacks to the *maquiladora* system. As the Mexican border cities become more and more crowded—attracting labor from all over Mexico—they also become more expensive to live in. Housing has become a major problem. The bare landscapes surrounding the modern American factories are dotted with *colonias*, clusters of one- or two-room shacks made of discarded plywood, plastic, and other factory refuse, with cardboard interior walls, dirt floors, a camp stove for cooking, and the barest of furnishings. As the northern Mexico winters are cold, many of the female workers send their children south to stay with relatives.

Food costs, too, are high in the Mexican border cities. The *maquiladora* workers have actually learned that it is cheaper to cross to the U.S. side and shop in one of the big American supermarkets than it is to buy food on the Mexican side. Even so, their wages cannot keep up with their living costs. In addition, protections against unsafe or unhealthy working conditions, which would be mandatory in the United States, are practically nonexistent in the *maquiladoras*. Also, employee benefits such as sickness or unemployment insurance and child care are rare.

It is doubtful that wages will ever rise high enough in the *maquiladoras* for Mexican workers to even distantly approach the living standards of their American counterparts. Nor is it likely that the Mexican government or the workers themselves (whose potential labor force outnumbers the available jobs) will ever ask for higher hourly pay. If they should, the industrialists of the prosperous nations might pull their plants out of Mexico. For there are numerous sites such as China, Taiwan, Indonesia, and countries in South America that already offer cheaper labor costs than those in Mexico.

ANOTHER EFFORT TO PLACE THE TWO NATIONS IN A CLOSER ECONOMIC balance has been the North American Free Trade Agreement (NAFTA), which took effect in 1994. The agreement was entered into by the United States, Canada, and Mexico with the goal of stimulating trade among the three nations by gradually phasing out tariffs and other barriers to trade such as taxes on raw materials or finished goods that increase costs. It was also hoped that the Mexican economy would prosper through NAFTA, ultimately diminishing the flow of immigration to the United States.

However, the changes called for under the agreement will take years

Life in the Mexican border cities is often one of squalor and hardship, because wages are too low to offset the high cost of living.

to realize, and it is too soon to determine the effects of this plan. For the present, it appears that the disparity in per capita wealth between Mexico and the United States will continue, as will the flow of illegal immigration.

The passage of the 1996 Illegal Immigration Reform and Immigrant Responsibility Act indicates that the United States government is still trying to control that flow. The act calls for stiffer penalties for *coyotes* caught

What are the conditions faced by some Mexicans who have remained in their native land?
Nearly one-fifth of the population has an income of less than $75 a year.

smuggling illegal aliens, and it increases the size and powers of the Border Patrol. It speeds the deportation process for illegal aliens and lengthens the waiting process for those applying to enter legally even if they are the relatives of citizens.

In spite of all efforts—including such outlandish suggestions as building a wall along the entire U.S.–Mexican border—people continue to enter illegally, "pushed" primarily, as they have been for decades, by the desire to escape limited economic opportunity in their homeland.

The Mexican population is close to 100 million and has been doubling every twenty-eight years. Mexico City, the country's crowded capital of 18 million, is choking on environmental pollution and is rife with social problems. Political corruption on the local and national level continues to plague Mexico, as does its unstable monetary system.

Economic growth has been slow and erratic in spite of the nation's rich natural resources and hardworking populace. The widening gap between the affluent and the rest of Mexican society creates public fear as a result of robberies, assaults, and kidnappings. More than 50 percent of the Mexican labor force is underemployed, their skills and time not being fully utilized, or unemployed, and nearly 20 percent of Mexicans earn less than $75 a year.

Some observers see the emigration of Mexicans as a safety valve, a system that serves as an antidote for economic frustration severe enough to lead to social upheaval. A new revolutionary scene in Mexico would surely create serious problems for its U.S. neighbor. As a result of these many "push" factors, the United States is today home to some five to six million undocumented immigrants, with about one million or more currently attempting to enter illegally every year and about one-quarter million succeeding in their effort.

Mexican Americans, here holding up the symbol of their homeland, make up nearly two-thirds of the Latino population of the United States.

Seven

The Mexican-
American Presence

HOW MANY PEOPLE OF MEXICAN ORIGIN LIVE IN THE UNITED STATES today? Census figures can tell us only part of the story because people living below the poverty line, lacking permanent housing, having limited education, and fearful of being detected as illegal aliens do not report. One or more of these conditions apply to between one-quarter and one-third of Mexican Americans, as well as to other Latinos dwelling in the United States—Puerto Ricans, Cubans, Dominicans, and Central and South Americans.

Mexicans, being in the majority, make up nearly two thirds of the Latinos in the United States, or about 23 million of the estimated total Latino population of 35 million.

Like other Latinos, Mexicans are settling in parts of the United States that are increasingly distant from their place of origin. They have established themselves in Washington and other parts of the Northwest, in the northern Midwest, in New York and New Jersey, and most recently in the Southeast. But most still live in the Southwest, especially in California where they make up more than 40 percent of the city of Los Angeles. Texas is second to California in the size of its Mexican population.

The large Mexican presence in California—more than 25 percent statewide—has led, over the years, to a variety of prejudicial measures. In 1978, the state's voters passed Proposition 13, which favored lowering property taxes. As *Parade*, the Sunday newspaper supplement magazine, reported that year, "Some Californians say their state is becoming 'Mexicanized,' that Hispanics constitute the largest single group of public-school students in their districts. They resent booming taxes to educate kids 'whose folks are probably illegal immigrants.' "

A later study showed that only 7 percent of illegal immigrants statewide had children in public schools. Yet, many Californians were willing to cut education funding even if it meant depriving their own children of quality learning.

Again, in 1994, 59 percent of California voters passed Proposition 187, known as the SOS or Save Our State initiative. The proposition was yet another measure that sought to deny social services to illegal immigrants, including educational opportunities for their children, because Californians felt that illegal aliens were a drain on the state's services.

This time, however, the courts put a stay on the referendum because of its severity, and it has not yet been activated. This delay was due to a widespread anti-187 campaign by Mexican-American activists, artists, and writers, and to a booming economy which was able to absorb large numbers of immigrant Mexicans without evidence of their driving down wages or increasing unemployment. An economic downturn, however, or a recession could possibly lead to more legislation like Propositions 13 and 187, in both California and elsewhere.

WHAT IS THE TRUTH—IN GOOD TIMES AND BAD—ABOUT MEXICANS WHO

Taking the oath of citizenship. Too often, Mexican Americans are automatically assumed to be illegal aliens rather than legal residents or U.S. citizens.

work in the United States, with or without proper documentation? Do they take jobs away from Americans? Are they "welfare bums"? How do they contribute to the economy of either the United States or Mexico?

The question of whether Mexican workers take jobs from Americans has already been answered in part. Often it is hard for employers to find laborers willing to do the backbreaking "stoop work" required in the produce fields. In addition, agricultural chores such as weeding onions, topping asparagus, pruning grapevines, and even picking tomatoes and peaches require a certain amount of farming know-how. Yet all too often such jobs run the risk of exposing workers to harmful sprays and insecticides. At the same time, it is the low wages they are paid that help to make American food among the cheapest in the developed world, taking a mere 8 percent out of the average family's budget.

101

Mexican Americans have also carved out for themselves an entirely new range of occupations. No longer confined to working solely in agriculture, mining, and railroading as after the "great" migration of 1910–1930, they have long since become part of an expanding middle class with considerable buying power. They own large and small businesses that number in the hundreds of thousands. There is no sector of the economy in which they cannot be found working alongside their Anglo counterparts.

What about the "welfare bum" charge? Is it really true that—as the proponents of Proposition 187 believe—Mexicans must be denied public health care, school lunches, and free education because they do not pay the taxes that support these services?

The answer is that Mexicans, even at the lowest economic level, do contribute to the local tax base every time they pay sales taxes on the purchases they make out of their earnings. Also, many illegal aliens have federal and state taxes withheld from their earnings and therefore contribute to social security. Although it is technically illegal to do so, Mexican workers who are unable to obtain a "green" card—the laminated identification card bearing a social security number and permitting one to work in the United States—will "share" the card of a documented worker, passing it around from one job applicant to another. Taxes will be collected and paid to the government for the workers claiming that social security number. The false cardholders, however, will never collect the social security tax they have paid into the system.

Lastly, how—if at all—do Mexicans benefit the economies of both their home country and their adopted country? Unlike immigrants from Europe or Asia, Mexicans in the United States may live only a few miles from Mexico. But even when the physical proximity is not that great, Mexico is still a bordering nation. Family reunions, cultural events, and shopping needs keep Mexicans in the United States in touch with Mexico and vice versa. Many Mexicans prefer to obtain the American products

The hope of a better life for the next generation—one of the many reasons Mexicans choose to leave their native land

they favor. At the same time, Mexican Americans often go back across the border for their shopping needs, as well as for doctor and dentist visits and for pharmaceutical items, which are cheaper in Mexico.

Whatever the reason for the busy traffic back and forth, there is no question that both economies derive some benefit. But beyond the daily exchanges that take place there are the efforts of individual Mexicans who work in the United States, either temporarily or permanently, for the purpose of sending money to their families back home. This bounty, which amounts to a very large sum annually, allows Mexicans, in turn, to buy many of the imported American goods that are popular south of the border.

WHILE AMERICANS MAY BE WILLING TO RECOGNIZE THE ECONOMIC BENefits that derive from the Mexican-American presence, they still often harbor feelings of cultural separatism. Anglo Californians, Texans, and others in the Southwest may live unthinkingly with Spanish place names for their cities, towns, and streets. They may enjoy tacos, guacamole, and the popular cuisine known as Tex-Mex. They may even enthusiastically join the Cinco de Mayo festival held by the Mexican-origin members of their community. But, in general, Americans tend to see Mexicans as family- and tradition-oriented to such a degree that they think of them as clannish. Mexicans, on the other hand, often feel that Anglos are selfish and individualistic, success-driven, and focused on material acquisitions. Mexicans who adopt these attitudes and lifestyles are unflatteringly called gringos by their neighbors.

Even young people, attending the same schools and sharing the same popular culture, often feel the strain of their different backgrounds. Anglo and Mexican youth may play soccer together, collect baseball cards and comic books, and enjoy the same popular music, TV, and computer games. But Mexican families may require more of a young person's free time than Anglo families. Sons and daughters are sometimes needed to bridge the gap between Spanish-speaking parents and the English-speaking world

The best way to educate the bilingual is an ongoing debate that especially impacts some Mexican-American students.

around them. Or they may be called on to care for young sisters or brothers, or to take an afternoon job.

Another factor separating Anglos and Mexican-origin students, as they move through school, is the scholarship-achievement gap. In spite of the efforts to "head start" Latino youth, they remain under-represented in programs for the gifted and in advanced-placement high school courses. As a result, high school graduation and college enrollment rates lag behind for Latinos.

As a group Latinos also rank disproportionately high in suspensions from school due to troublemaking and other antisocial activity. Educators understand that historical trends are at work here. Young people who feel undervalued, either by their families or society, tend to become alienated and to act out their frustrations. So there is much more work to be done through culturally sensitive educational programs.

FINALLY, IN THE UNITED STATES IN THE TWENTY-FIRST CENTURY, LATINOS will become its largest minority. As Mexican Americans make up two-thirds of that group, their presence will increase accordingly. Probably the principal thing to recognize is that, just as Mexicans were part of the American past, they are also part of its future. The first Mexicans on American soil did not cross an ocean or even a border. They were simply *here* when a major segment of the United States was carved out of half of Mexico.

The United States needs, too, to take some responsibility for having encouraged the great waves of Mexican immigration in a number of ways. It bolstered the greedy and dictatorial regime of Porfirio Díaz, which led directly to the first major thrust northward. It has since manipulated the Mexican labor force by valuing and encouraging it in time of need, yet subjecting it to callous deportations whenever the U.S. job market has tightened.

Now however—more than one hundred and fifty years after the present U.S.–Mexican border was drawn—it is time to see Mexican Americans as more than wanted, or unwanted, fruit pickers and day laborers. They have become an economically diverse people. They are blue-collar workers and white-collar workers. They are students, teachers, university professors, and educational administrators. They are women of achievement, as well as men.

They are artists and writers, sports and entertainment figures, astronauts and scientists. They run small businesses and large corporations. They are involved in civic, cultural, social, and political affairs, and in

Tradition lives on in the next generation of Mexican Americans. With her face painted like a skeleton and wearing a ring of roses in her hair, this girl prepares for her community's celebration of the Day of the Dead.

labor management. They are mayors of cities, governors of states, senators and representatives on the state and federal level, and members of the president's cabinet.

In short, it is time to stop thinking about Mexican Americans as "them." Historically, economically, and politically, they are "us."

Bibliography

de Varona, Frank. *Latino Literacy: The Complete Guide to Our Hispanic History and Culture*. New York: Henry Holt, 1996.

Dinnerstein, Leonard, Roger L. Nichols, and David M. Reimers. *Natives and Strangers: A Multicultural History of Americans*. New York: Oxford University Press, 1996.

Ehrlich, Paul R. *The Golden Door: International Migration, Mexico, and the United States*. New York: Ballantine Books, 1979.

Garcia, Richard, compiled and edited by. *The Chicanos in America 1540–1974: A Chronology and Fact Book*. Dobbs Ferry, NY: Oceana Publications, 1977.

Gonzales, Manual G. *Mexicanos: A History of Mexicans in the United States*. Bloomington, IN: Indiana University Press, 1999.

Gutiérrez, David G., ed. *Between Two Worlds: Mexican Immigrants in the United States*. Wilmington, DE: Scholarly Resources, 1996.

Langley, Lester D. *MexAmerica: Two Countries, One Future*. New York: Crown, 1988.

Maciel, David, and María Herrera-Sobek, eds. *Culture across Borders: Mexican Immigration and Popular Culture*. Tucson, AZ: University of Arizona Press, 1988.

Martínez, Oscar J. *Fragments of the Revolution: Personal Accounts from the Border*. Albuquerque, NM: University of New Mexico Press, 1968.

———. *Troublesome Border*. Tucson, AZ: University of Arizona Press, 1988.

———, ed. *US-Mexico Borderlands: Historical and Contemporary Perspectives*. Wilmington, DE: Scholarly Resources, 1996.

McWilliams, Carey. *North from Mexico: The Spanish-Speaking People of the United States*. New York: Lippincott, 1949.

Natella, Arthur A., Jr. *The Spanish in America 1513–1979: A Chronology and Fact Book*. Dobbs Ferry, NY: Oceana Publications, 1980.

Perl, Lila. *Mexico: Crucible of the Americas*. New York: William Morrow, 1978.

Shorris, Earl. *Latinos: A Biography of the People*. New York: W.W. Norton, 1992.

Notes

p. 19, Valdez, Luis, and Stan Steiner. *Aztlán, An Anthology of Mexican American Literature*. New York: Knopf, 1972.

p. 29, Moquin, Wayne with Charles Van Doren. *A Documentary History of the Mexican-Americans*. New York: Praeger, 1971.

p. 39–40, Lewis, Oscar. *Pedro Martínez: A Mexican Peasant and His Family*. New York: Random House, 1964.

p. 44–45, Beeson, Margaret, Marjorie Adams, and Rosalie King. *Memories for Tomorrow*. Detroit: Blaine Ethridge Books, 1980.

p. 54, Bustamente, Charles J., and Patricia L. Bustamente. *The Mexican-American and the United States*. Mountain View, CA: Patty-Lar Publications, 1969.

p. 80–81, Cantarow, Ellen. *Moving the Mountain: Women Working for Social Change*. Old Westbury, NY: The Feminist Press and McGraw-Hill, 1980.

p. 90, Morrison, Joan, and Charlotte Fox Zabrusky. *American Mosaic: The Immigrant Experience in the Words of Those Who Lived It*. Pittsburgh: University of Pittsburgh Press, 1993.

Further Reading

NONFICTION

Brimner, Larry Dane. *A Migrant Family*. Minneapolis: Lerner, 1992.

Galarza, Ernesto. *Barrio Boy*. Notre Dame, IN: University of Notre Dame Press, 1971.

Hoobler, Dorothy, and Thomas Hoobler. *The Mexican-American Family Album*. New York: Oxford University Press, 1994.

Krull, Kathleen. *The Other Side: How Kids Live in a California Latino Neighborhood*. New York: Lodestar, 1994.

Ochoa, George. *The New York Public Library Amazing Hispanic American History: A Book of Answers for Kids*. New York: John Wiley, 1998.

FICTION

Cisneros, Sandra. *The House on Mango Street*. Houston: Arte Público Press, 1984.

FILMS ABOUT IMMIGRATION AND MEXICAN-AMERICAN LIFE

El Norte (1983)

Born in East L.A. (1987)

The Milagro Beanfield War (1988)

Stand and Deliver (1988)

My Family/Mi Familia (1995)

Index

Page numbers for illustrations are in **boldface**.

111